Short ish w in north Devon

Robert Hesketh

Bossiney Books · Launceston

All the walks in this book were checked prior to printing, at which time the instructions were correct. However, changes can occur in the countryside over which neither the author nor the publishers have an control. Please let us know if you encounter any serious problems.

Second edition 2009
First published 2004 by
Bossiney Books Ltd, Langore, Launceston, Cornwall PL15 8LD
www.bossineybooks.com
Copyright © 2004 and 2009 Robert Hesketh
All rights reserved
ISBN 978-1-906474-11-9

Acknowledgements

The maps are by Nick Hawken, cover design by Heards Design Partnership.
Boots on the front cover kindly supplied by The Brasher Boot Company.
All photographs are by the author or from the publishers' own collection.
Printed in Great Britain by R Booth Ltd, Penryn, Cornwall

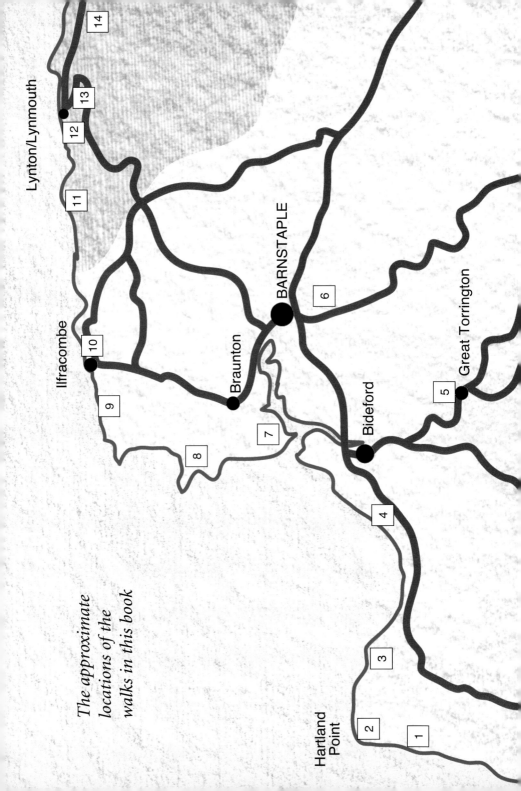

The approximate locations of the walks in this book

Introduction

This is an invitation to some of England's finest coastal and moorland paths, a walker's paradise. High cliffs and rocky shores, rolling hills cut by fast-flowing rivers and steep wooded valleys – North Devon is endlessly enjoyable.

At 4-9 km (2½-5½ miles) all the routes in this book can be walked in a morning or an afternoon. The time you need will depend on how fast you walk and how interested you are in what you see – and that will include historic inns and churches, waterfalls and rock formations.

Safety (please take seriously!)

Walking the coast path is safe and trouble free – if you are prepared. In the first place the cliff paths are not fenced. Do not go to the edge and follow any diversions away from eroding paths. Secondly Devon weather can change suddenly. As well as enjoying a generally mild climate, we also experience high winds – especially south of Hartland Point – and fogs. It has also been know to rain (and *rain*) here.

Please do not go without good walking boots and suitable clothing. Drinking water, map and compass, plus waterproofs and an extra layer are equally essential, together with a comfortable rucksack. Many, including myself, add a walking stick and food to the list.

Access

Beaches, and unenclosed areas of Exmoor, are generally open access. But please keep to paths over enclosed farmland and in woodland, use (and close) gates as appropriate, and keep dogs under control.

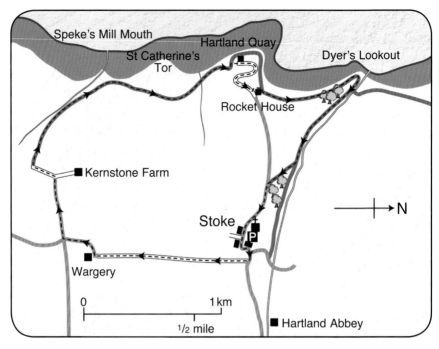

Walk 1   Stoke and Hartland Quay

Distance: 8.5km (5¼ miles)   Time: 2½ hours
Character: Splendid coast path walking with great views.
Dramatic rock formations, the coast's largest waterfall and a church
of exceptional interest. Especially photogenic. Some steep gradients.

Start from the small car park by Stoke church (SS 235247). With your back to the church, turn left. Walk past Stoke Barton Farm and take the next lane on the right, past the front of Rose Cottage. After 200 m the lane becomes a track, UNSUITABLE FOR MOTORS. Walk on for 900 m. At Wargery, bear right onto the tarred lane. On reaching Kernstone Cross, turn right signed KERNSTONE. At the end of the lane bear left through the gate and follow the PUBLIC FOOTPATH FOR SPEKE'S MILL MOUTH. Walk past the cottage onto a grassy path. When it joins a track, keep right and walk on.

The waterfall is almost hidden away on your left, behind a wooden fence. The best view (see page 32) is obtained by taking a short path that leads down from a gap in the fence. Take extreme care if you do this.

Return to the coast path, which climbs steeply before levelling off. Continue over a ladder stile and follow the path downhill, to walk behind St Catherine's Tor, once the site of a medieval chapel – hence the name. At the far side of the tor is a smaller waterfall, which may run dry in summer. Keep right here, up a stony track

On reaching the car park, turn downhill for Hartland Quay, with its hotel, shop and small museum. The cliffs, with their fantastically folded rocks and the saw-toothed formations stretching out into the turbulent sea, are forbidding indeed. It is hard to believe that it was once a thriving quay. In fact it dates from Queen Elizabeth's time and continued in use until late nineteenth century storm damage. Hartland Quay handled a variety of cargoes, notably lime to feed three kilns and malt for the malt-house. A small bank issued notes until 1833.

Follow the track uphill for 150 m and rejoin the coast path at a sign on the left. Push uphill to the Rocket House where life-saving gear was once stored. Go through the gate as signed and continue to Dyer's Lookout.

The path descends and curves inland to a junction. Don't cross the stile, but press ahead on the signed public footpath, STOKE, which follows the wood inland above the Abbey River. It emerges into a field. Keeping the edge of the wood on your left, and the church tower ahead, continue uphill to meet a lane. Turn left and follow the path parallel to this lane over a series of stiles to Stoke's exceptionally interesting church, St Nectan. The tower is, at 39 m (130 ft), the highest in north Devon and a daymark for shipping. Inside are a Norman font and a variety of monuments and brasses, as well as a wonderful ceiling and carved screen. The Pope's Chamber, reached by a small door in the north wall, is a small museum.

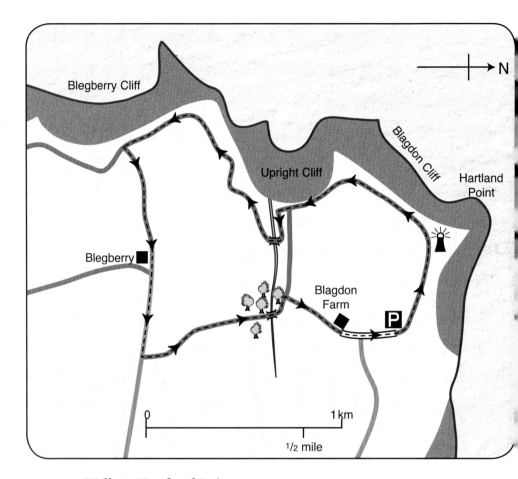

Walk 2 Hartland Point

Distance: 5km (3 miles) Time: 1 1/2 hours
Character: The dramatic rocky scenery of the Atlantic coast starts here.
The views both ways along the coast and across to Lundy are excellent.
There are some demanding gradients. Seals and porpoises are often
seen on incoming tides.

From Hartland Point car park (SS 235275) take the coast path west, signed HARTLAND QUAY. Walk to the gate of the lighthouse, built in 1874 and manned until 1984. It is closed to the public. See it and the wreck of the *Joanna* (1982) from the viewpoint, a short diversion from the path.

   Loop back on to the well-beaten path. Follow it around the field edge to a stile. Note the memorial (2002) to the *Glenart Castle*, a hospital ship torpedoed by UC 56 in 1918.

Beyond Blagdon Cliff and Upright Cliff, the path descends to a waterfall. Unless you wish to short cut by taking the signed path to Blagdon, follow the path upstream and cross the footbridge. Continue uphill via the stepped path. At the top, turn right on the coast path.

At the fingerpost ahead, follow the coast path through a gate, over a stile and down steps. The path turns left and then climbs up via steps to Blegberry Cliff. Follow the coast path as indicated along the edge of the field, admiring the saw-toothed rocks below.

At the far end of the field, at the point where the coast path begins to descend towards Blackpool Mill, turn left onto PUBLIC FOOTPATH BLEGBERRY. Follow the edge of the field inland for 150 m. Turn sharp left and head uphill between two fields. At the top of the rise, turn right onto a broad path and head straight for Blegberry.

Just before reaching this very interesting and historic farm, note the well house and pump house. Built of stone, they bear the dates 1657 and 1950. Blegberry's chimneystack is dated 1634 and the plasterwork inside 1627. The garden wall dates from the Civil War and has an observation platform and firing holes for muskets. Blegberry may be the site of the fortified house that Alan of Hartland built in 1202.

Walk through the farmyard and into the lane. 300 m ahead, turn left at the public bridleway. This pleasant green lane descends to a brook. Cross the footbridge. Bear right at the path junction and push uphill to Blagdon. Walk into the lane ahead and continue to the car park.

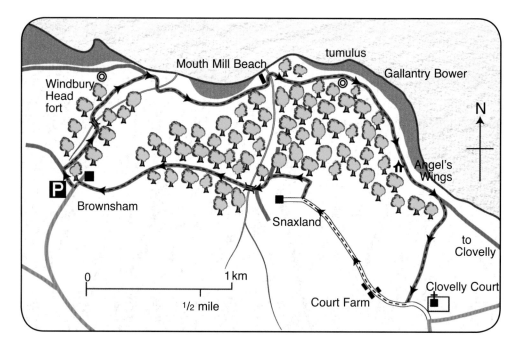

Walk 3 Brownsham and Gallantry Bower

Distance: 8 km (5 miles) Time: 2 3/4 hours
Character: Superb coastal views compensate for tough gradients.
Much of the walk is in woodland, so there is shade on a hot day.

Park at the National Trust's Brownsham car park (SS 286260). Study the excellent display map. Take the footpath which leads out of the car park, towards the Beckland Valley. Enter the wood by a gate and, 10 m further on, keep right, signed WOODLAND WALK COAST PATH. Turn left at the next path junction, WOODLAND WALK WINDBURY HILL FORT, down to a footbridge. Cross the bridge and turn right, WINDBURY HILL FORT COAST PATH, then after 40 m sharp left, WINDBURY HILL FORT, and in another 30 m right, up steps, signed COAST PATH.

The path winds and zigzags uphill. Part way up is a bench – a marvellous viewpoint. From the bench turn right, downhill, MOUTH MILL. At a junction turn left, MOUTH MILL. Cross a footbridge. Follow the zigzag path uphill to Brownsham Cliff. Cross the stile and keep left along the field hedge, as signed. Follow the path down to Mouthmill Beach and its limekilns. On the rocky beach is Blackchurch Rock, with its two natural archways.

Cross the stream and follow the track on the far side, uphill. Look out for the yellow coast path arrows, taking you on a zigzag course to

8

Gallantry Bower. Rest at the Angel's Wings, a carved wooden shelter built in 1826.

Continue on the coast path for another 400 m. At a junction first keep ahead, then fork right, TO THE CHURCH. Where another track crosses, walk ahead as indicated by a white arrow. Continue through Winsley Wood to a T-junction. Turn right, PUBLIC BRIDLEWAY, and walk past Court Farm with its handsome bow front and sundial. Walk on between the farm buildings, slightly uphill through a gate and farmyard, beyond which there's a PUBLIC BRIDLEWAY sign. Follow the track through a field, then between hedges, then into another field with a hedge to the left and a downslope on the right. At the end of this field the main track continues to a house – Snaxland. Don't follow it. Turn right, keep the hedge on your left and walk down the slope for 100 m to a PUBLIC BRIDLEWAY sign. Turn left through the wooden gate and walk ahead, with the wood on your right.

Only 100 m further on, the path dips into the trees to a metal gate. Follow the bridleway ahead and downhill as indicated by the blue arrow. At the junction turn left onto a smoother track, and in 100 m turn right. Continue on the bridleway through the woods, ignoring side turnings. The track climbs slowly to Lower Brownsham Farm. Turn left on to the tarmac lane, and 100 m ahead turn right into the car park.

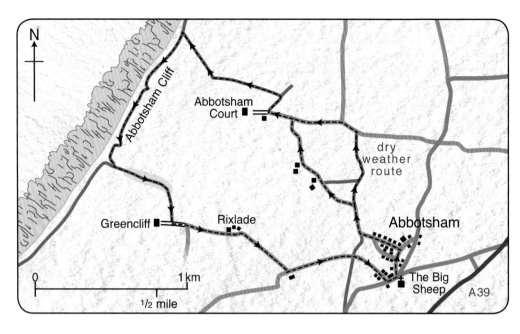

Walk 4 Abbotsham

Distance: 5.7 km (3½ miles) Time: 1¾ hours
Character: Quiet lanes and footpaths lead to Abbotsham Cliff and
extensive views stretching from Hartland to Baggy Point and across to
Lundy. A fairly gentle walk, with ascents but none of them very steep.

Start from Abbotsham church. Take the lane opposite the church, signed to the THATCHED INN. Just before reaching the Inn – a cob and stone building of considerable age with interesting period photographs of Abbotsham – turn left along PUMP LANE. (An iron pump stands on the left.)

Walk ahead at the lane junction and follow the lane when it curves sharp right out of the village. When the lane curves left, you have a choice. If the weather has been dry recently, continue ahead down an unsigned stony track. Follow it downhill to damp ground, then up to the lane at Rickard's Down. Turn left. Ignore the lanes to Cornborough and Abbotsham and continue to the end of the lane.

However, this track is liable to flooding, so after wet weather it may be best to stay on the lane and rejoin the main route by turning left at the next junction.

At the end of the lane, turn right, PUBLIC FOOTPATH ABBOTSHAM CLIFF. Turn left over a stile at the next PUBLIC FOOTPATH sign. Cross the next stile and continue for 200 m, then cut diagonally right as signed, across a large field to a stile.

Turn left, COAST PATH BUCKS MILLS. Follow the coast path for 1 km. Please note that the cliff is unstable – keep away from the edge and heed warning signs. At Green Cliff, turn left through a gate, PUBLIC FOOTPATH ABBOTSHAM. Follow the path through newly planted woodland to a concrete farm track, and turn left along it.

The track joins a tarred lane. Continue ahead and walk past Rixlade to a lane junction. Turn left, ABBOTSHAM, and follow the lane back to the village. Turn left back to the church.

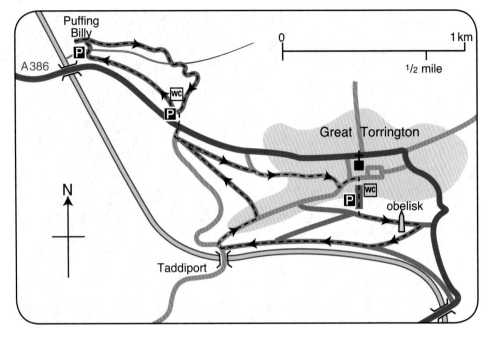

Walk 5   Great Torrington and the Commons

Distance: 5.4 km (3 1/4 miles)   Time: 1 1/2 hours
Character: Well surfaced paths along the side of the Torridge Valley
with excellent views.

Park in the Sydney House car park in South Street. Leave at the far end and turn left to join the path under the walls of Torrington Castle, which was built in 1139 and destroyed in 1228. The walls we can see are early Victorian. The town's commanding hilltop position, with its sweeping views of the Torridge Valley, made it a natural defensive position, but this did not prevent Parliamentarian forces from successfully attacking Torrington in 1646.

Follow the path past a row of seats and downhill to the Waterloo Obelisk. Bear left onto the Monument Path to descend further. Take the first path on the right (SLIDING ROCK PATH). At a fork keep left, downhill to river level. Continue with the river on your left to Taddiport Bridge. Don't cross; turn right by the tollhouse.

At the Torridge Inn, turn right up the steps into Mill Street. Follow the street uphill and turn left up the alley between numbers 86 and 84. Continue, pushing uphill and diagonally left. Torrington Commons is an area of 140 hectares (350 acres) donated for the benefit of the poor by Baron Fitzherbert of Torrington in the 12th century. On reaching the road, turn right and walk uphill to the Commons car park. There

is a helpful map of the Commons on the wall of the public conveniences.

With your back to the public conveniences, proceed through the picnic area from which a well-beaten path descends parallel to the road. At the foot of the hill keep right. Ignore the Alexander Path and take the tarmac path ahead. Turn left at a T-junction of paths, and cross the stream by a small concrete bridge. Turn right after the bridge and follow the valley side uphill. After 280 m keep right along the narrower path, then right again down a track and back over the stream. Follow the stony track as it winds uphill to the car park.

Re-cross the road and head towards Taddiport. After 130 m turn left onto the footpath signed for Great Torrington. Join a road and continue. Bear left through a gate into and through Rack Park, then straight on into South Street.

To visit the historic centre of Torrington continue past the car park and turn left at the Market House. Like the nearby Town Hall, this is early Victorian. Just beyond is St Michael's Church. Royalist soldiers were imprisoned here after the Battle of Torrington, which virtually ended the civil war in the West. Unfortunately, gunpowder was stored in the church and killed 200 prisoners when it exploded. The church was rebuilt, still in the Gothic style, in the 1650s and the handsome tower and spire (a landmark for miles around) were added in 1828.

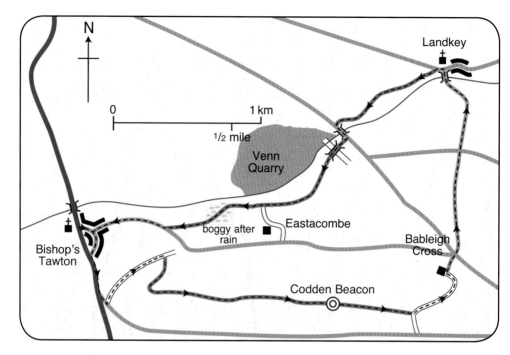

Walk 6 Bishop's Tawton and Landkey, near Barnstaple

Distance: 8 km (5 miles) Time: 2 1/2 hours
Character: Footpaths and quiet country lanes. The circuit includes
Codden Beacon (189 m, 620 ft) a magnificent viewpoint, as well as two
interesting villages each with a historic church and a brace of pubs.

Park next to Bishop's Tawton parish church, noted for its crocketed octagonal spire, unique in Devon, and for the sanctuary ring set in its door. Turn right from the church, walk up the main road and bear left into Village Street, past the 15th century Chichester Arms and the Three Pigeons, also 15th century and an inn since 1623.

Turn left to rejoin the main road and after 150 m turn left into the lane signed COBBATON AND CHITTLEHAMPTON. Immediately, turn sharp left and take the first track. Walk steeply uphill past the quarry gate, and after 250 m fork right, where the footpath diverges from the main track.

Walk uphill on the broad stony track for 300 m, ignoring side turnings. Turn sharp right (at SS 574298). Continue uphill till you meet a wire fence; this leads up to Codden Beacon and a memorial to Caroline, wife of former Liberal leader and local MP, Jeremy Thorpe.

Use the directional compass on the monument to spot landmarks, then take the downhill path to the east. At a gate this joins a broad

14

track just beyond a small car park. At a junction of tracks turn sharp left, taking the track downhill between hedges to a lane; this bears right in front of a house, and on to Bableigh Cross. Take the second lane on the left, signed LANDKEY.

Landkey church has a typically Devonian tower with battlements and gargoyles. Bear left (or right if you want to explore the village) and take the lane for Barnstaple. After 80 m, turn left at the Tarka Trail footpath sign. Go through two gates and follow a well-beaten path through a wood by a brook.

At a stile turn left onto the lane and cross the bridge. Follow the Tarka Trail waymarks, turning right 50 m beyond the bridge. The path leads around Venn Quarries and over an arched bridge. Proceed to a PUBLIC FOOTPATH sign and turn immediately right; cross a stile and continue along the signed trail, past a pair of stiles and along the woodland edge by a brook. (This section becomes boggy after heavy rain: you can divert left at the pair of stiles, up a grassy then tarmac track to the lane, then turn right along the lane back to Bishop's Tawton.) Follow the field edge from the next stile to the far field corner, where the next stile is half hidden, some 30 m up the slope to your left.

Cut diagonally across the next field in line with the telegraph pole ahead. Exit at the top corner and continue in the same line across a further field to a stile. Turn right and follow the lane back to Bishop's Tawton.

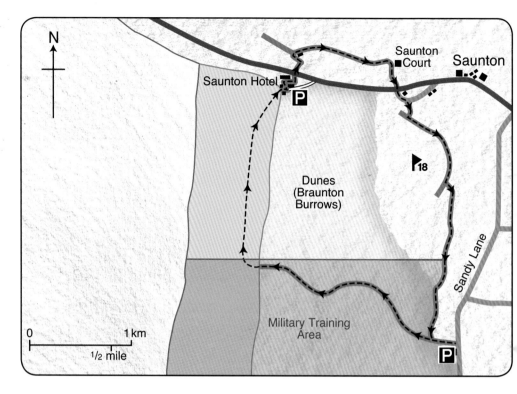

Walk 7 Saunton Sands and Braunton Burrows

Distance: 9km (5 1/2 miles) Time: 2 1/2 hours

Character: Slightly longer than most of the other walks in this book, but very easy walking, except for one long ascent. (This can be avoided, but to do so involves 400m on a busy road, so we do not recommend it.) Massive dunes, a massive beach, and an amazing view, make this a memorable walk. For the best beach walking, avoid the highest point of the tide.

Whilst the public is generally very welcome in the Burrows, they are also used as a military training area. On very rare occasions red flags are flown and the area is closed for live firing. You may see soldiers or military vehicles – just keep out of their way, and don't touch any debris.

Start from the Sandy Lane car park (SS463350). Take the track signed NO UNAUTHORISED VEHICLES, then shortly COAST PATH PUBLIC BRIDLEWAY. At a path junction, continue ahead, unsigned, and follow the main broad sandy track as it winds through the dunes.

At a T-junction, turn right then immediately keep left. Ultimately you will emerge onto the beach.

Turn right along the beach for 1.8 km (over a mile). Turn right up a ramp to beach facilities (shops, food, toilets, car park) then turn left, COAST PATH.

Climb the concrete path to the hotel, then continue ahead on a narrow path leading to the right of the tennis courts and round to the main road.

Cross directly over, taking great care, then bear right over a stile, PUBLIC FOOTPATH FOR ALTERNATIVE COASTPATH ROUTE AVOIDING ROAD. Climb to a stile, then up the field to a signpost. Turn right, PUBLIC FOOTPATH SAUNTON COURT. A track leads over the hill then down to Saunton Court. Follow the driveway down and out to the main road.

Cross directly over into a minor road. At a corner, continue ahead COAST PATH BRIDLEWAY, through grassy dunes.

Go through a gate and turn left. Follow the broad and well-signed COAST PATH PUBLIC BRIDLEWAY across a golf course, then into the military training area.

Reaching a T-junction, turn left, COAST PATH, back to the Sandy Lane car park.

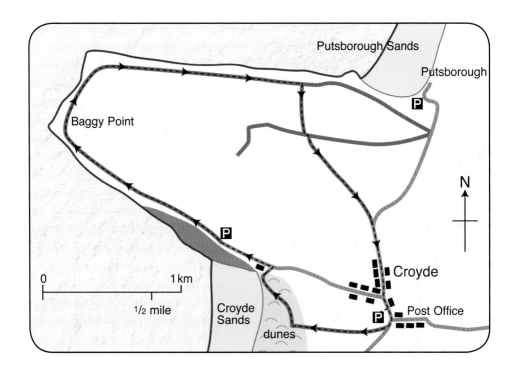

Walk 8 Croyde and Baggy Point

Distance: 7.5 km (4 1/2 miles) Time: 2 hours

Character: Well surfaced, gently graded coast path. One stretch is often muddy, requiring good footwear. Superb views, fascinating geology and bird watching add to the interest.

From the car park in the centre of Croyde, turn right and almost immediately right again from the Billy Budd pub.

Follow the signed footpath towards the beach. Ignore the first right turn, which leads through a park, but bear right towards the sand dunes. Cross the stream ahead by the second footbridge.

Keep to the path as it leads up the steps and over the dunes, which have been partially fenced off to promote regeneration of the marram grass.

At the end of the dunes turn right at the footpath sign. Walk up the lane past the public toilets and turn left, BAGGY POINT. Follow this lane past the National Trust carpark and take the path signed BAGGY POINT. The National Trust has given this path the Rolls Royce treatment – it is broad and smooth.

Baggy Point is an SSSI (Site of Special Scientific Interest) because of

its fascinating shale and sandstone geology and varied birdlife, including colonies of gulls, raptors and larks. Also of interest beside the path are some suitably outsize bones from a whale washed up in 1915.

On a clear day, Lundy and the Welsh coast are visible from Baggy Point. From the Point, turn uphill for 150 m and continue left, past the observation pole, along the Coast Path for 2 km. This involves a gate and three stiles.

Some 130 m beyond the third stile, take the signed footpath on the right. This path begins by following a field hedge on the right, to a stile. Continue ahead, cross a second stile and turn left into an enclosed green lane (this is the muddy section).

Follow the lane downhill past Cherry Tree Farm to a lane junction. Ignore the footpath on your right and continue along the lane ahead into Croyde.

Opposite Moor Lane, join the footpath on the left. This runs parallel to the road and leads to the start.

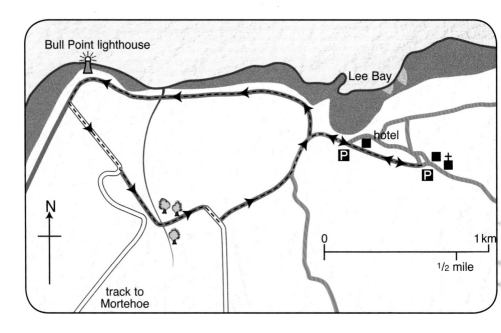

Walk 9 Lee Bay and Bull Point

Distance: 5.7 km (3 1/2 miles) Time: 1 3/4 hours
Character: Exhilarating cliff-top path with fine views, but steep
gradients. Delightful inland paths back to Lee.

Park opposite the church (or alternatively use the car park by the beach). Turn left out of the car park and after 50 m fork left past the Grampus Inn, named after the dolphin-like creature that blows out air and water. Continue ahead on a signed public footpath, but ignore the footpath on the left over a stile.

Turn left up the lane and walk steeply uphill for 350 m. Turn right up steps at the Coast Path sign. The path (rich with daffodils, primroses and then bluebells in spring) leads up, dips then rises steeply, only to drop and rise again. Each time it offers a grander view of the high and marvellously folded cliffs.

Push on to Bull Point lighthouse, built in 1879 and rebuilt in 1972 after a cliff fall. Although the lighthouse was automated in 1995, the keeper stayed on as the attendant. From the lighthouse, turn left up the tarred track signed MORTEHOE.

After 500 m, go through the gate then leave the track and take the narrow footpath signed LEE & BENNETTS MOUTH. The path descends steeply. Bear right at the bottom signed LEE & MORTEHOE. Walk on to a footbridge, keeping the brook on your left. Cross over onto the Lee footpath and press uphill through the trees.

Follow on through a field, with the hedge on your right and a small standing stone on your left. Bear right over a stile as signed. 150 m ahead, turn left over a stile (it's beside the middle gate) signed LEE. Cross a second stile at the end of the field and continue along an enclosed path. On reaching the tarred lane, turn left for Lee. Retrace your steps to the car park, past Cliffe Garden (seasonal opening), noted for unusual plants which thrive in the shelterd microclimate..

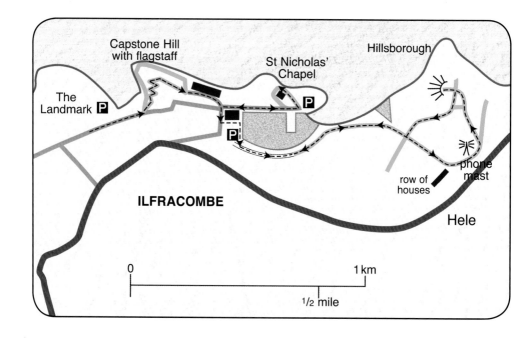

Walk 10 Ilfracombe Harbour and cliffs

Distance: 5.6km (3¹/₂ miles) Time: 1¹/₂ hours
Character: Clearly marked cliff paths (partly tarred) and
harbourside streets.

Ilfracombe's superb setting amidst the cliffs turned it from a small fishing town into North Devon's leading Victorian resort. A little shabby in places but still proud, Ilfracombe remains predominantly Victorian in buildings and atmosphere. It was, however, an important medieval port. When Edward III besieged Calais in 1346, six ships and 79 men were sent from Ilfracombe, whilst Liverpool sent just one ship. Local vessels traded to Wales and as far as the Mediterranean in Tudor and Stuart times and many were built in Ilfracombe.

The 18th century pier was widened in 1825, 1829 and again in 1874 as tourists flocked in. Up to six paddle steamers lay up there. One can still sail to Wales and to Lundy, and fishing remains important.

Start from the Tourist Information Centre in the Landmark, Ilfracombe's arts and entertainment complex which features two starkly modern cones of white brick. Turn left along the front past the shingle inlet, then bear left and climb the zigzag path to the flagpole on Capstone Hill. You will see the Landmark one side and the harbour the other. Descend towards the harbour. Walk along Capstone Road (the street nearest the sea), pass between the Sandpiper Inn and

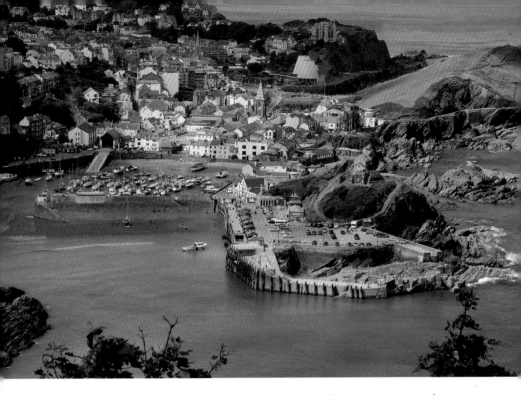

the Royal Britannia Hotel, along the Quay. Pass the Aquarium and the Harbour Master's Office and take the path to your left, climbing Lantern Hill to visit St Nicholas' Chapel (open May-October) which is a quaint and fascinating building well worth a visit. St Nicholas is the patron saint of sailors and this was a place of worship, study and pilgrimage – and refuge from Lundy pirates.

The Chapel dates from the early 1300s, but Lantern Hill showed a fire to guide sailors before that. Secularised at the Reformation, it became a dwelling but continued as a lighthouse; it has been restored and houses Victorian press cuttings and photographs, and a few ship models.

Return to the harbour, turn left at the Royal Britannia Hotel and left again into the quayside carpark. Follow the quay around the harbour, then follow the COAST PATH signs, which will lead you beside a small golf course and up Hillsborough. When you reach a crossing of paths with HELE BEACH to your left, go straight on. Just beyond the phone mast and a row of houses the path bends left. Take the first fork left and push on uphill (ignoring a path to your left) to the viewpoint where a viewing table explains the magnificent panorama.

Now follow the winding path downhill, turning right at the crossing of paths, and retrace your steps past the harbour to the car park.

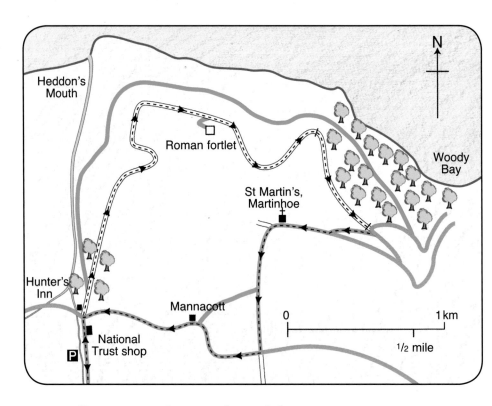

Walk 11 Hunter's Inn and Martinhoe

Distance: 7 km (4 1/2 miles) Time: 2 hours
Character: Well graded and surfaced path with wonderful views of coast, Exmoor and South Wales. Quiet country lanes. One long but steady climb, and one steep descent.

Park at the National Trust car park near Hunter's Inn (SS 655480). Walk down the lane to Hunter's Inn and take the path to the right of it, signed for HEDDON'S MOUTH WOODY BAY. When the path forks take the upper route, signed WOODY BAY. This is well graded and surfaced, as usual with paths on National Trust land: it was once a carriage drive between Hunter's Inn and Woody Bay, which explains why it is so wide.

Curving round Hill Brook, the track leaves Heddon's Mouth Cleave (a Devon word for a cliff-sided valley) and turns east along the coast. Keep to this track for 2.5 km, but take care not to miss the signed path up to the Roman fortlet on Martinhoe Beacon, 250 m (800 ft) above sea level.

The fortlet was in use from about AD 50 to AD 70. It enabled a garrison of some 80 soldiers to keep watch on the warlike Silures of South

24

The walk takes you along the carriage drive on the right of the photograph; the official coast path can be seen at a lower level

Wales, whose hilly homeland stretches before us, whilst the vista to the east shows Cock Point, the Valley of Rocks and Countisbury. The Silures were not subdued by Rome until AD 75. A double earthwork can be traced in the grass: excavations revealed two timber barracks, a workshop and a store, as well as field ovens and a forge. (The booklet available at the National Trust shop gives fuller details.)

Return to the main path the way you came and turn right. Walk on to a gate and continue along the top edge of Woody Bay's woods. Go through another gate at the end of the woods, which leads into a lane.

Immediately – before setting foot on the tarmac! – turn sharp right, FOOTPATH MARTINHOE, cutting back along a narrow uphill path to reach another lane. Turn right into Martinhoe. The chancel and tiny tower of St Martin's Church are some 700 years old.

Turn right out of the churchyard, and follow the lane left and uphill. There is a footpath on the right (see sketch-map) which provides a short cut, but we found it difficult walking and preferred the lane. After 800 m at a junction turn right, and follow this lane downhill past Mannacott Farm, dropping steeply to Hunter's Inn and a well-earned pint.

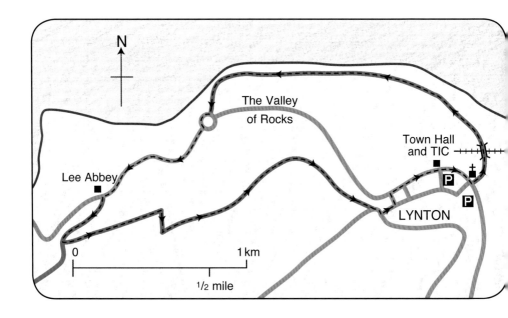

Walk 12 Lynton and the Valley of Rocks

Distance: 6.6 km (4 miles) Time: 2 hours
Character: De luxe coastal footpath, short lane section, then return by an inland path with excellent views of the exceptional Valley of Rocks.

Facing the Lynton Tourist Information Centre at the Town Hall (SS 719495) turn right and head downhill. Turn left in front of the church, down North Walk Hill, past hotels and signs for VALLEY OF ROCKS. Fine views of the Foreland open up.

Cross over the cliff railway into an avenue and on to a de luxe footpath, with wonderful views of South Wales.

At a path junction, continue ahead, signed COAST PATH, CASTLE ROCK.

This leads to the dramatic Valley of Rocks. Now a dry valley, it once contained a large river which left considerable rock deposits of 'head'. Coastal cliff erosion dismembered the valley. Spectacular tors and other frost-riven features mark its sides. Possibly these were the result of glacial action. Such action was exceptional in Devon, which lay just south of the ice sheets that covered most of Britain during the last Ice Age.

At the roundabout, bear right to join the lane ahead. It is signed COAST PATH (ALONG ROAD). Only 100 m ahead, divert right onto the footpath parallel to the road. Regain the road 500 m ahead.

North Walk, Lynton

Continue to Lee Abbey, then bear left onto the footpath signed LEE ABBEY AND LYNTON.

The track enters Six Acre Wood. Ignore the first unsigned path on the left. Take the second turning left BRIDLEWAY SIX ACRE CROSS, thus turning sharp left, almost doubling back.

The path climbs gently to a fingerpost. At this point take the path signed LYNTON VIA SOUTHCLIFFE. Walk uphill and on through a gate.

After 200 m, the path forks. Take the upper path, leading to the top of the ridge by a steep zigzag. Follow the ridge path on: there are great views of the Valley of Rocks and sometimes walkers meet the renowned wild goats.

The path descends to a junction. Keep right and 200 m ahead left to join a lane. Turn left and downhill, signed LYNTON.

Turn left into Crossmead. Join Lydiate Lane and follow signs for the TOWN CENTRE which will bring you to the Town Hall and Tourist Information Centre.

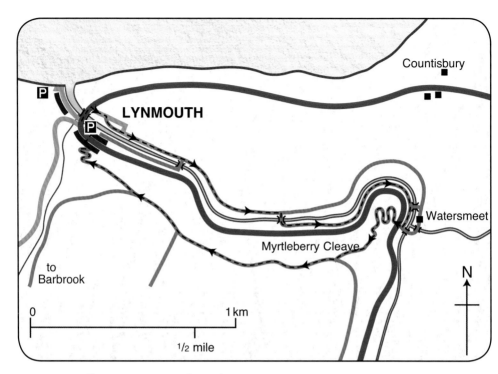

Walk 13 Lynmouth and Watersmeet

Distance: 6.7 km (4 1/4 miles) Time: 2 1/2 hours
Character: A superb riverside and ridge walk with dramatic views,
by well-marked footpaths. Two steep ascents, two steep descents. This
walk could be dangerous if the river has risen after very heavy rain.

Park at Lyndale Cross car park in Lynmouth (SS 724494) and cross
the road bridge at the lower end. Turn right along Tors Road and
walk uphill, parallel to the East Lyn. After 100 m, bear right through a
public garden and follow the bankside route signed to WATERSMEET.
It is well surfaced and well graded. Walkers have the choice of using
bridges to explore either bank for much of the way.

The best time to appreciate the East Lyn is after heavy rainfall, when
the waters roar over its tumbled boulders. On a calm summer's day it
is hard to believe that the East and West Lyn flooded so suddenly and
violently in August 1952 that the ensuing spate, equivalent to more
water than flows down the Thames in three months, swept away cars
and houses and killed 34 people. Over 9 inches (225 mm) of rain had
fallen on Exmoor in only two days – a record one hopes will never be
matched.

Hoar Oak Water joins the East Lyn by 'Watersmeet', a Victorian

28

hunting and fishing lodge, now a National Trust tea room, shop and information centre. From the tearoom, cross back to the opposite bank by two wooden footbridges. Turn right, then after 20m left and uphill on a zigzag path. After a further 20m, turn sharp right at the sign LYNTON AND BARBROOK OVER THE CLEAVES.

On reaching the road, cross straight over and take the path opposite, LYNTON, LYNMOUTH VIA THE CLEAVES. This path winds up to Myrtleberry North Camp, an Iron Age fort with its ramparts clearly delineated. Follow the path uphill through the camp and up to the top of the steep slope ahead. Steps relieve the steepest part of the climb. Marvellous views open out.

Spare a thought for the Lynmouth lifeboat crew. One January night in 1899 they were telegraphed to aid the *Forest Hall*. The seas were so high they could not launch from Lynmouth so, with the aid of 20 horses, they hauled their heavy lifeboat more than 22km (14 miles) over the 400m (1300ft) high hills opposite you, and launched at Porlock to aid the vessel and crew.

At the top of the slope turn right onto the TWO MOORS WAY and follow the signs for Lynmouth. The path zigzags downhill, then zigzags up Oxen Tor. Take the right-hand path downhill, following signs LYNMOUTH, with yet more zigzags to ease the steep descent.

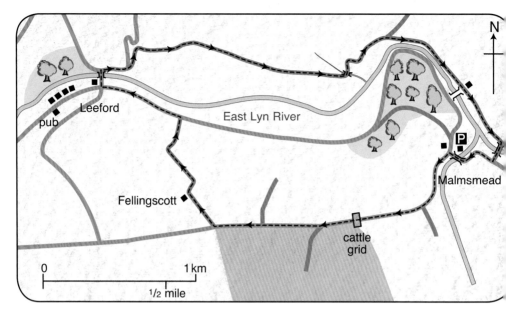

Walk 14 Malmsmead and Brendon

Distance: 7.1 km (4 1/2 miles) Time: 2 hours
Character: Pleasantly varied: moorland views, footpaths via fields
and riverbank, quiet country lanes. Literary associations with
R D Blackmore's novel, Lorna Doone *(1869).*

Park at Lorna Doone Farm, Malmsmead (SS 792478) with its gift shop, refreshments and public conveniences. Take the lane signed FELLINGS-COTT SLOCOMBESLADE TIPPACOTT, which climbs, goes round a bend, then climbs again. Cross a cattle grid and continue uphill. Ignore the first bridleway right (even though it is signed for BRENDON.)

Look for the point where, on the left side of the lane, the open moor gives way to enclosed land. Turn right here, through a wooden gate, onto a bridleway. (At the time of writing this bridleway was being renovated and the turning was unsigned.)

Walk down through two fields to Fellingscott Farm. Keep to the track to the right of the buildings. Go through the wooden gate ahead, turn right and walk past a barn, then turn left at the next gate and walk ahead with the fence on your left. Continue across the next field to a fence, then turn right and walk steeply downhill with the fence on your left.

Turn left onto the tarred lane and continue to Leeford Green Cross. Turn right and cross two bridges. Note the old high-arched packhorse bridge a few metres downriver. Turn right and 200 m ahead climb the ladder stile on the right, signed MALMSMEAD.

Follow the well-beaten path uphill past the first of a series of yellow waymarks. The path soon bears right and continues upwards, levelling out to follow the upper contours of the East Lyn valley, of which there are fine views. Continue ahead through waymarked gates and over a stile.

After crossing a footbridge, turn left and follow the old track ahead as it bears sharp right and uphill. 100 m ahead, bear right through a hunting gate – *not* the field gateway. Bear right and downhill for MALMSMEAD and OARE.

On reaching the river, bear left and upriver past a house with a private bridge. Do not cross here, but use the second bridge, which has a blue waymark. At the lane, turn right. Walk on past the field study centre (limited summer opening) to the start.

Some other Bossiney books you may find useful

Exmoor Pub Walks, Robert Hesketh
North Devon Pub Walks, Robert Hesketh
Shortish Walks on Exmoor, Robert Hesketh

Exmoor, a Shortish Guide, Robert Hesketh
Lynton and Lynmouth, a Shortish Guide, Colin Croxford

Devon's Geology, Robert Hesketh

*The
waterfall at
Speke's Mill
Mouth, see
page 4*

Phone numbers of Tourist Information Centres

Barnstaple (01271) 375000
Bideford (01237) 477676
Braunton (01271) 816400
Combe Martin (01271) 883319

Ilfracombe (01271) 863001
Lynton (01598) 752225
Torrington (01805) 626140)
Woolacombe (01271) 870553